Make a Change

Rhonda Lynn Rucker
with James "Sparky" Rucker
Illustrated by Brock Nicol

whites only

PELICAN PUBLISHING COMPANY
GRETNA 2017

*The word "Pelican" and the depiction of a pelican are
trademarks of Pelican Publishing Company, Inc., and are
registered in the U.S. Patent and Trademark Office.*

ISBN: 9781455622757
E-book ISBN: 9781455622764

Printed in Korea
Published by Pelican Publishing Company, Inc.
1000 Burmaster Street, Gretna, Louisiana 70053

First and foremost, I give all my love and appreciation to my husband, James "Sparky" Rucker, to whom this story truly belongs. My heartfelt gratitude also goes to Ann Schwarz, Richard Willey, and Terry Caruthers, who have each helped me grow as a writer. I also salute Brock Nicol, who made this book come alive with his fabulous illustrations. Finally, special thanks to Erin Classen and all the hardworking folks at Pelican for their help and support. —RLR

To my beautiful wife, Anka. Thank you for all the years of love, encouragement, and support. —BN

Mama shook her head as she gazed at the Whites Only sign above a water fountain. "One of these days," she said. "One of these days, *what*, Mama?" I asked.

Grand Opening

"Things are gonna change, that's what." She grabbed my hand. "Come on, Marvin. Let's find the boys' department." I tripped, trying to keep up with her.

Big, bold signs marked Grand Opening were plastered on the walls inside Rich's, the new department store in Knoxville. "Don't they have a toy department?" I asked.

Mama ignored me and found a rack of pants. I leaned against a table. I hated shopping. Mama was never satisfied until I had tried on everything in the store. This time was no different. By the time we finally found a pair, my legs felt like rubber. Then we went downstairs.

At the bottom of the escalator, I smelled it. French fries. "Hey, look!" I said. "They've got a grill!" Inside, a boy munched on a hamburger. A waitress carried a tray of sandwiches with fancy toothpicks perched on top. My stomach growled.

"I'm really hungry," I said, adding a quiver to my voice. I knew good and well we couldn't sit down at most of the restaurants in town. They had those Whites Only signs. But this was a new place, so maybe it was different.

Mama looked uncertain but walked inside. I ordered a sandwich and french fries, and she paid the cashier. While we were waiting, I sat on one of the swivel stools at the counter and turned back and forth.

A white man with greasy, gray hair watched me. He wasn't smiling. Another fellow, young enough to be the other's grandson, sat next to him, eating a sandwich. The greasy grandpa slowly set his hamburger down. He rose from his chair and pointed a shaking finger to the sign behind the counter: Seating for Whites Only.

"Boy, your kind ain't supposed to be sitting down in here," the old man growled.

About that time, the waitress handed us a bag with my sandwich. Both men watched as we left.

"Why won't they let us sit down?" I asked Mama for the millionth time.

She never had a good answer. "When some people look at us, all they see is our skin color," she said. "They think they're better than us." Mama shook her head. "One of these days . . ."

But I wasn't sure things *were* going to change.

During dinner that evening, I talked about Rich's. Saundra, my older sister, lifted a wedge of cornbread from the skillet. "People at school were talking about that. They said there's a mass meeting Saturday at Reverend Crutcher's church."

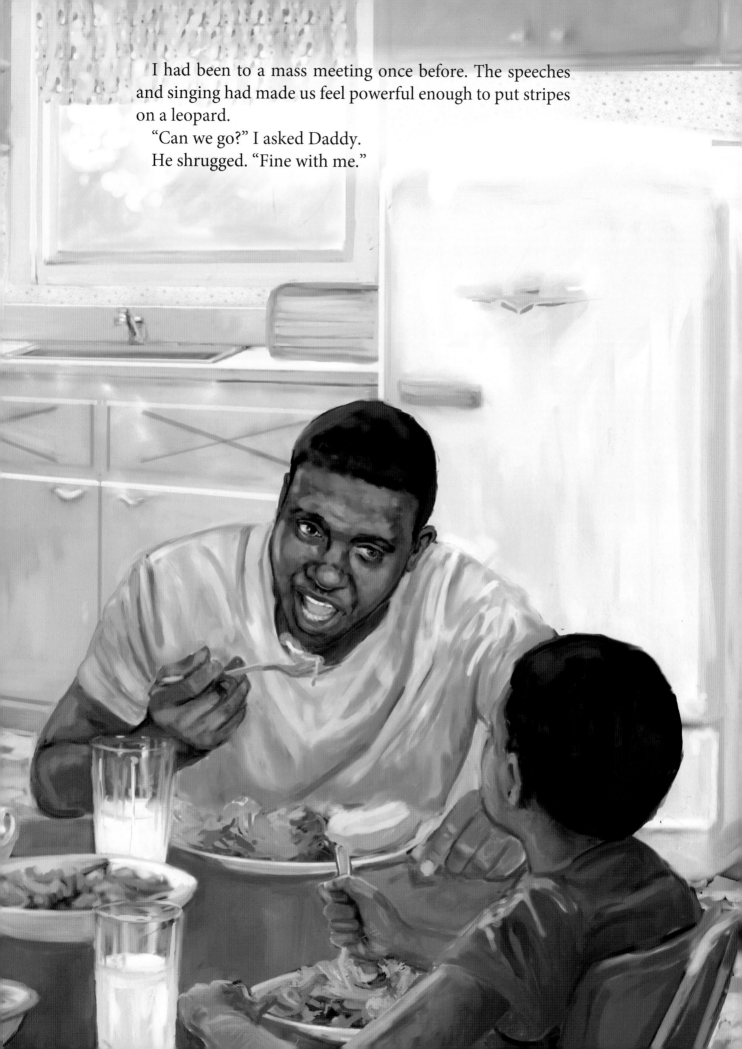

I had been to a mass meeting once before. The speeches and singing had made us feel powerful enough to put stripes on a leopard.

"Can we go?" I asked Daddy.

He shrugged. "Fine with me."

At the meeting, one person after another talked about the lunch counter at Rich's.

"I'm never gonna shop there again!"

"Let's do more than that. Let's picket!"

"But we gotta get permission from the city."

"Then let's get permission!"

I knew what it meant to picket a store—people marched outside with big signs to scare off shoppers.

Reverend Crutcher's voice thundered in the sanctuary. "We will *not* fight back—even if they throw stuff at us or hit us!" At the end of the meeting, everybody sang, "Don't you hear the Spirit say 'make a change'?"

But a few days later, we got bad news. The city wouldn't let us picket. After all the bold talk at the mass meeting, we had failed. I decided I could live without the french fries at the new grill.

One evening, Saundra surprised me at the dinner table. "Somebody at school said they're having a pray-in at Rich's this Saturday."

"A pray-in?" I asked.

"Everybody kneels outside and prays," Mama explained. "Keeps people from going in the store."

"Works as well as picketing," Daddy said. "And they can't stop us from praying."

"I can't go," Saundra said, frowning. "I've got band practice."

Daddy grunted. "I've got to work."

This wasn't looking good for me, and I wanted to be able to sit down in restaurants. "Can I go, Mama?"

"No, it's too dangerous," she replied.

"But Reverend Crutcher said sometimes you gotta *make* change happen."

Mama raised her eyebrows. "I'll think about it."

On Saturday, Mama woke me up. "You feel like praying today?"

Later that morning, we walked up Locust Street to Rich's. Lots of people were there. After Mama found a spot for us, we kneeled on the cold, hard concrete. She closed her eyes. I folded my hands and bowed my head, but I was too scared to shut my eyes.

Sure enough, a white man came walking toward us. And it wasn't just any white man—it was the younger guy I had seen at Rich's eating with his grumpy old grandpa. I glanced at my mother, but her eyes were still closed. With my hands folded in front of me, I balled my right hand into a fist, ready to fight.

The man came within two feet of me—and then his face broke into a smile. He waved and said, "Howdy!"

My right hand relaxed, and I stared at him, unable to speak. Mama opened her eyes wide. "Hello."

The man nodded at me. "Okay if I kneel next to you?"

By then, my voice had recovered. "Yes, sir." He kneeled and folded his hands.

I realized I had made a mistake. I had assumed he would be mean. But I also realized something else.

Change had already begun.

This story is fiction, but it is based on my husband's true-life childhood experience at a 1960 pray-in in Knoxville, Tennessee.

At that time, African Americans and whites could not attend the same schools, live in the same neighborhoods, or even use the same restrooms. Many of the downtown lunch counters, including the one at Rich's Department Store, did not allow African Americans to sit down and eat.

Rich's opened its Knoxville store in 1955, five years before the June 1960 protests began. Marchers carried picket signs in front of several businesses, hoping to discourage customers. Sometimes white people woul[d] shout insults and hurl objects at the protester[s]. After a month of demonstrations, sever[al] counters were finally opened to all customer[s] including African Americans. However, Rich['s] announced that instead of allowing blacks t[o] sit down, it would have a stand-up snack ba[r] for everyone. A few months later, Rich's close[d] its Knoxville store.

The incident in this book changed m[y] husband's life. It made him realize that a[ll] whites were not full of hatred and that som[e] were even working for change.